When The Silence Echoes

Aruvi Saha

BookLeaf Publishing

India | USA | UK

Presentation by *BookLeaf Publishing*

Web: www.bookleafpub.com

E-mail: info@bookleafpub.com

ISBN: 9789363304017

First edition 2024

To those who think they lack the strength to face life with all its pain and its joy. You don't. It's just waiting for the right time to show itself.

PREFACE

Deep into that darkness peering, long I stood there wondering, fearing,
Doubting, dreaming dreams no mortal ever dared to dream before;
But the silence was unbroken, and the stillness gave no token,
And the only word there spoken was the whispered word, "Lenore?"
This I whispered, and an echo murmured back the word, "Lenore!"
Merely this and nothing more.

-Edgar Allan Poe, "The Raven"

Table of Contents

The Dawn's Serenade

Darkness everywhere, the night devours all,
Memories of light and joy become small,
As it sneaks up like a stealthy assassin,
Fills minds up with indecision.
Heavy shadows flow in, our pretentious allies,
As the thick fog blankets us, making a perfect
disguise.

But it won't last, won't take long to fade,
All of it will be washed away, all the doubts and
the hate,
When the gloom dims and the darkness lightens,
The heads bowed down look up, their faces
brightened.
As colour bleeds into the dark skies,
The sorrow dies and the smiles arise.

The vibrant hues streak across the top of the
world,
Golds and oranges and crimsons intertwine and
twirl.
They waltz in harmony, their beauty increased,
The sky a canvas, prettier than any manmade
masterpiece.
A gentle breeze blows, music to their dance,
Their choreographer looks on from above in an
awed trance.

And then like a sapling, the sun peeks up,
Gently warming us with joy and trust.
Shy like a newborn babe, it tentatively appears,
Its innocent beauty filling our eyes with stunned
tears.
It slowly moves over our heads,
Unknowingly, its presence in our hearts it
embeds.

Eyes open as the first rooster crows,
One by one they look up, their reverence only
grows
For the miracle that is nature's painting,
As the last of the shadows leave, slowly fading.
The world awakens, rejoicing as the night is
gone,
Embracing the light, the birth, the beauty of the
dawn.

Those We Forget About

Sitting on the corner of a road, a girl wears a
threadbare dress,
Her eyes tired and her hair a mess,
She can't be older than thirteen,
Still has so much of the world to see,
But she never even had an opportunity to truly
live,
As she clutches hope with trembling fingers, a
weakening grip.
And so she sits in the cold,
Shivering profusely, her story has so much left
to unfold.

A mother and her young son beg for food on the
street,
Their bodies thin and their throats dry from the
heat,
She cradles him close to her chest as they move,
Hoping with all her heart that their lives will
improve.

And so it is with so many of us,
Leading our own lives, we forget about the
hurting ones,
Those who did nothing to end up like that,
Those who didn't deserve a single attack.
A child, a brother, just specks of dust in this
wide, wide world,
A mother, a sister, never getting a chance for her
life to unfurl.

And so it is, unfairness walks hand in hand with
birth,
Dancing a bittersweet dance, finding pleasure in
the pain on Earth.

Memories

I live a life with ease,
Ups and downs with every heartbeat,
Some moments to light me up, some to bring
tears,
Some lightweight causing contentment, other
storms unravelling my fears.

A beautiful love in a grain,
A vein of hurt pulsing in the body, carving out
pain.
A gentle trust to embrace,
A seed of humiliation sprouting disgrace.

A cascade of seconds flow into a life,
Hurting and healing, they linger in the back of
my mind.
So many little drops of water in an ocean,
Each tiny bead containing a molecule of
emotion.

Every day new droplets are made,
Every night, each bubble in the present fades.
Each life, seconds build into legacies,
Each fate, years collide into dynasties.

Our present is our past, our future our present,
So much to treasure, so much unpleasant,
The moments that await us are soon our history,
The days we cannot get back, they're lost in a
memory.

Birth Of A Mother

She lays in a blissful sleep,
A soft smile on her face, her breaths gentle and
deep,
Her little hand holding the hem of her quilt,
Her serene face, free from sorrow and guilt.

I gaze at her in wonder,
The happiness in me is louder than thunder,
As I reach down to brush a stray curl from her
face,
Her tiny body so peaceful, my mind can think of
nothing but praise.

The light movement makes her shift,
Will she ever know how she anchored me when
I was a boat adrift?
My thoughts encompass nothing but her as she
slowly turns,
To give her the world and more, my heart
yearns.

Her mouth opens in a small 'O' with a soft
yawn,
One day I'll tell her how to my life, she is the
dawn.
Her big eyes open, blinking up at me,
Swaddled in blankets, she is the source of my
blissful ecstasy.

As she smiles up at me, I muse about fate,
How could I possibly find her in this winding
maze?
She holds her arms out to me,
As I gently bring her to my chest, our hearts a
satisfied symphony.

My daughter snuggles close
And looks at me with a trusting face,
A fierce protectiveness blooms, as the new
mother in me
Steps up to take my place.

A Bright Flame

Somewhere far, in an ordinary life,
He lived with constant joy and strife,
Uncertain whether his heart rang true,
He marvelled at the world, at family and
strangers too.

When his mother spoke,
Quiet, unassuming, and always in a peaceful
tone,
Her words made sure to be heard,
In her voice, the lines between meekness and
authority blurred.

His father, a reserved mountain of might,
Showed him the importance of self-esteem and
pride.
With his confident strides and wisdom,
He taught him the power in emotional freedom.

He saw the epitome of grace in his sister,
So poised, her head raised high no matter the
nearby whispers,
A perfect soul, radiant in her imperfections,
Her light adorned him with her affection.

Quiet wit was his brother's element,
His thoughtful words and decisions, his
testament,
His interactions inspired those around,
The way he could see through a soul without
making a sound.

Then his friend, whose heart reached out,
Touching the world with fingers of empathy,
never having a single doubt.
The way she smiled without regret,
Made him want to have the same mindset.

The faces he saw, the hearts he touched,
Made him long to be better, his desire he
clutched,
To soak in the warmth of every passing candle,
To be the brightest he could, the most he could
handle.

And so he walked through his life,
Through all the joy and the strife,
His mother's strength, his father's spirit,
embodied in him,
His sister's pride, his brother's wit, filling him to
the brim,
His friend's purity, his family's resilience,
driving him to be better,
His own joy, his beauteous curiosity, staying
with him forever.

To Say Goodbye

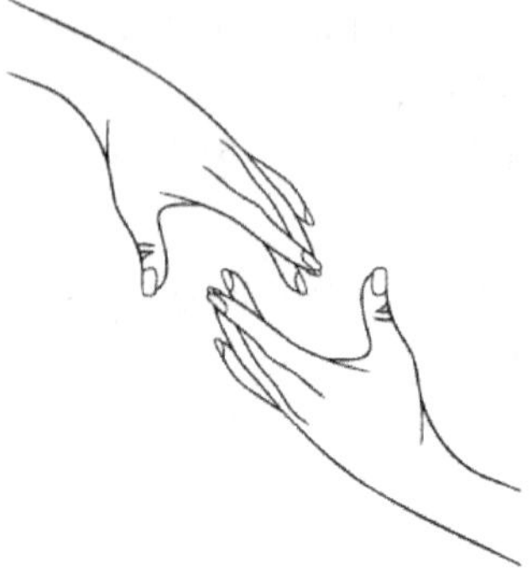

She looks up at the night sky dotted with stars,
Such a beautiful view but her heart's in shards,
Hugging her knees close to her chest, she looks
so vulnerable,
As she screams out into the darkness, her voice
cracking and unstable,
A tear rolls down her cheek and drips onto the
grass,
She wipes it away ferociously, her heart now a
twisted, mangled piece of brass.

At the young age of twelve, she never deserved
it,
Her father couldn't have left her, the memory of
his laugh still moonlit,
Just a while ago he was laughing beside her,
And now, he was among the stars, her tears
becoming a blur.

She shakes with the force of her heartbreak,
Her desperation dissolves and her screams fade,
Till she's trying to hold her soul together with all
she has,
Breaking apart from her pain, her heart bearing
thousands of unfixable cracks.

Reaching out to the sky, she whispers questions
that will never be answered,
Her mind numb from shock and a piece of her
heart shattered,
She knows she will never be the same,
He won't come back no matter how many times
she calls out his name.

She gazes up at the stars,
Her watery eyes undermining the depth of her
scars,
But she knows there is no one to blame,
After all, fate is merciless and life is just a game.

She rises to her feet, stumbling a little,
Her actions slow and her movements brittle,
And although her tear-stained face can't explain
why,
She will always love her father, but the time has
come to say goodbye.

Arise

It rises, swooping in the sky,
Majestic body in the air, soaring high,
Breathtaking in hues of fire,
Fills the land with a touch of glory, a beautiful
desire.

Delicate feathers fluttering in the breeze,
Gliding above, it moves with ease,
With the flame and water, it is one,
So proud, fears it has none.

It beats its strong wings fast,
Of what is to come, it is aghast,
For its days are over, it can find no cover,
It cannot recover, nothing can stop this, nothing
whatsoever.

It falls down, its life reaching an end,
Burning and writhing, this it cannot fend,
And soon ashes are all that's left,
Its days done, its life to the sidelines swept.

Yet after a while, it rises as a child,
So small, those who thought it died, smile.
An embodiment of immortality,
Legends say it shall live for infinity.

Oh Phoenix, mighty Phoenix, glorious in your
light,
A forever inspiration of hope, so beautiful, so
bright,
All shall know of your resilience,
All shall dream of the legendary light of your
brilliance.

For the cycle of birth and death is unavoidable,
But the constant renewal of spirit is
indestructible.
Oh Phoenix, mighty Phoenix, your life is your
own,
You will live, die, and hope, lonely but never
alone.

Love And Loss

Love and loss, two delicate entities,
Converse in whispers under the lamp's glow,
So similar, yet with different personalities,
Peas of the same pod, grief is something they
both know.

Like twins they exist,
One to bring joy – the other to cause pain,
When one is there, the other cannot be missed,
When one isn't, the other doesn't remain.

Like yin and yang, like black and white,
They survive in harmony,
Like the sun and moon, like day and night,
Together, they create a bittersweet symphony.

One to bring your guard down,
To keep you safe, fill you with ecstasy,
To never give you a reason to frown,
To give the illusion of a forbidden fantasy.

The other to teach you how to heal,
Building your walls up, putting your wounds in
a sling,
To remove naivety, your ability to foolishly feel,
To prove trust to be a precious thing.

In the heart's vicious dance, both strike true,
Their care holding your soul beaten black and
blue,
In their arms they cradle you,
One whispering sweetly, the other giving you
life's harsh view.

Love and loss, two delicate entities,
Part ways on the lonely street,
Their job accomplished for your heart's
necessity,
Soon they'll meet again, breaking and tuning
another soul's beat.

A Sliver Of Pain

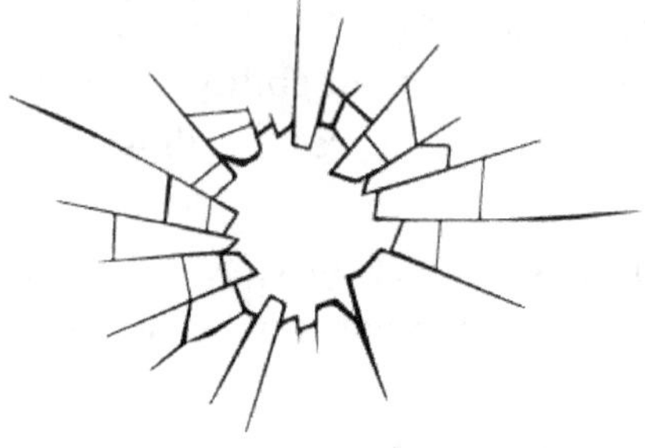

Weeping silently, his head bent low,
He sits in a corner, his monsters' masochistic
grins a blow,
Overcome by pressure and anxiety,
His battered soul cannot find sanctuary
Within his mind, where all the devils reside,
They look down upon him, broken and bruised,
satisfied.

Gasping, he shakes with the onslaught of his
tears,
Guess the pain was buried inside him all these
years,
He put on a brave face, pretended he was okay,
As all the angels left and his demons were there
to stay.
Now they applaud his unrelenting pain,
With each moment leaving an irreplaceable
stain.

All his doubts resurface in his mind,
Asking "Will I ever heal with time?"
They weigh him down with an invisible weight,
Is the pain just imaginary, or is it fate?
He sits there, helpless and hurting,
He prays to feel alright, his heart burning.

Eventually he stands, pushing down the hurt,
Locking it away, his feelings he diverts,
He stitches a smile onto his face,
Smart enough to hide away his permanent
disgrace,
And unpauses his "happy" life,
Nobody will ever know how that happiness is a
lie.

A Daisy

A bright spot of colour, a small burst of beauty,
She stands unwavering like a sentry on duty,
Her shade so vivid, her body so slender,
So small yet she adds to the world a slice of
splendour.

Friendless in miles of grey, she doesn't mind;
To all the chaos and the storms, she remains
blind,
An insignificant size having a significant impact,
Wanderers from their pensive thoughts she
distracts.

Her slim stalk stays upright,
Her unassuming posture filled with might,
As her unfurled petals bloom with pride,
Exposed for the world to see, her allure has no
reason to hide.

The sun himself adorns her with his light,
The stars all blink at her in awe in the night,
The wind caressing her soft leaves,
The world her audience, she performs a subtle
dance with nothing to grieve.

Every day, something to say, she speaks through
her motions,
Every night, she stands tall and bright, her
purpose encompassing oceans.

Let It Go

I try and I try, to keep them appeased,
A tiny bit of relief inside me if they seem
pleased,
With the way I walk, the way I talk,
The way they influence every action of mine,
From the way I stop, to the way I even shop,
Each thing I do seems pressurised.

Lately, I don't feel happy when with me they are
content,
Their intrusive comments just another thing I
wish I could prevent.
Exhaustion fills me, down to my bones,
Their demands from me become another
buzzing noise,
Whatever I do, their criticism will pelt me like
stones,
So why should I try, to have a perfect mind and
a perfect poise?

I'm not trying to please them any longer,
To me, their words always seem intended to
smother.
They will never be happy enough with what I
do,
Their reactions painting my lonely heart blue.
So I won't try again,
Enough is enough, who cares if it offends them?

My life is in my hands, my destiny just for me,
My wishes only mine to grant, my future is
finally free.

Voices

The world spins, everything vague,
My mind writhing, my smile fake,
I wear but a costume of joy in pretence,
A relaxed face with a heart so tense.

In my head, their voices are drowned out by my
own,
So sarcastic, it rips me, flesh to bone,
A bully in my head that can never leave,
A part of me I will always grieve.

Brutal and piercing, she mocks my flaws,
A constant reminder that I am not enough, I
wish I could hit 'pause',
Her face my mirror, her mind my twin,
Her heart beating with my veins, her voice
digging deep under my skin.

Stuck inside, she fills me with thorns,
My own soul glaring at me with scorn,
Mocking me with every step I take,
Smirking at my failures, a desperate ache.

Her body my own, I am her,
The beast trapped inside Beauty, it's all a
throbbing blur,
Her soul is mine, I am she,
Is it possible to break up with someone who was
always meant to be?

Her Innocent Strength

Under your feet, she reposes in a deep slumber,
Her eyes closed, her breaths a gentle thunder,
The rolling hills her curves, the rippling stream
her hair,
The resilient roots winding through her limbs
with care.

The birds chirp, the branches curve, acting out a
welcome,
The trees sway, the mules bray, a languorous
greeting well-spun,
For her rest has ended, some wrongs amended,
and she flutters open her eyes,
Brown and green hues, a serene blue, they
crinkle into a smile.

She raises her head and looks around,
Utters a contented sigh, a soft sound.
She rises to her feet, naked in her innocent
splendour,
But if she wanted, she could end the world with
a single tremor.

Bare feet cushioned with moss as she strides
forward,
The world beneath her feet, the universe at her
fingertips, her subjects move to adorn her.
The time has come; she takes her throne,
The almighty queen holds her head high —
proud, regal, and all alone.

The Lens Of Life

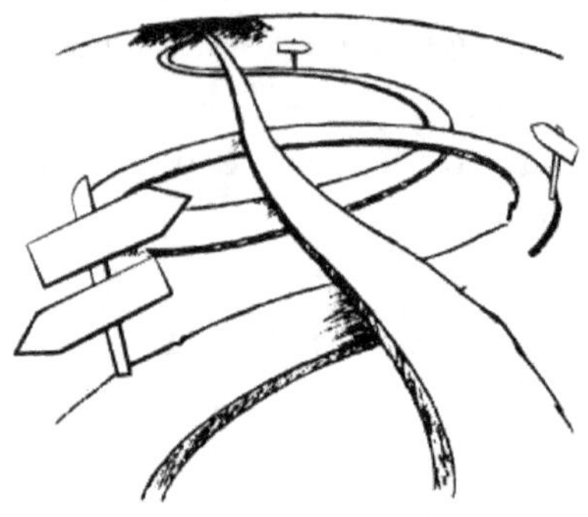

I know this will all end someday.
One day, I will realise
This is all over, and looking back on it,
I'll laugh and cry with my memories.
And thinking of this, I can't deny my fear;
That fright of not doing enough in this world,
Of not having enough meaning in this world.

But to bare my soul is to show vulnerability,
And hence, I can only open all doors here, where
nobody knows,
And it won't show my instability.
Soon all this comfort will merge
Into the unknown, never traversed before,
And with no knowledge of where to go.

But maybe that's life—learning to wander aimlessly
Through the fog and with no lamp to guide.
Yet, when you are on the brink of giving up,
Maybe the beauty lies in there always being
That one little spark to convince you
To breathe a little slower,
To walk a little further, and
To hold your head a little higher.

His Last Words

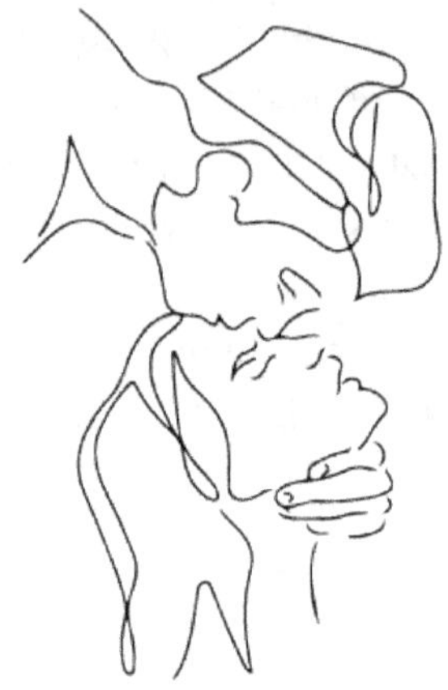

I recall the early days of my life,
The little boy for whom protecting people was
his passion, his drive,
He grew older, but that never left him,
He wanted to learn how to protect, instead of
being a victim.
And so he did, joining the army,
Until the vast battlefields were all he could see.

As I lay there, I mused deep in thought,
Were my decisions what I wanted after all?
Many would shake their heads in regret,
But I wouldn't change a thing, not even to
prevent what lay ahead.

Shivering to inhale, I think of my mother,
Broken-hearted when she would find out, her
heart plundered,
And my father with his easy smile,
Standing still after hearing the news, the light
gone from his eyes.
And then my wife, the thought of her pure grief,
Gives me more pain than the bullet ever could to
me.

But I refuse to think of the hurt,
Even though it threatens to drown me, as I'm
submerged;
So I turn my mind to better days,
To the younger me, laughing outdoors under the
Sun's rays,
To a childhood filled with love and care,
Where I could share anything with my family,
my soul laid bare.

And then, when I met the woman who I could
love endlessly,
Her steady heart and tender smiles were all that
were needed for me.
And lastly when I found out about our unborn
child,
Into skyscrapers was the ecstasy in me piled.

My blood soaks into the ground underneath,
My life flowing out of me as I desperately try to
breathe,
In my last moments, I cling on to these
memories,
As the emotionless breeze carries away my faint
pleas.

Try as I might, I cannot change this,
In a scorching desert, my memories are my
temporary oasis.
Gasping for air, I draw in a rattling breath,
Preparing myself for the inevitable death.

Eventually, the world dims and fades,
I steel myself; I will not be afraid.
With my last bit of energy, I scream out a phrase,
Hoping it will reach those I cannot erase.

From my limp mouth slips out a sorry,
So much feeling and desperation packed into
that one apology.
I close my eyes, my body is spent,
I wish they knew that I thought of them till the
very end.

Ballad Of The Soul

This feeling inside me, this overwhelming
emotion,
Full of regret, betrayal, and self-hating devotion,
Of the times I messed up, the times I failed,
The times I shattered inside, and in my heart, all
those broken trails.
Each moment I hurt, every second I bled,
Too many to count, but again that's how life's
led.

The other side of my soul, the one that's content,
Rejoices in the pleasures of life's little moments.
Be it falling in love or trusting a friend,
It always sees a silver lining, tracing each
brilliant fragment.
No matter how small, no matter how
camouflaged,
There's a beauty in living, never to be
sabotaged.

Then there's anger, a burning blaze,
It starts from a spark, till everything's engulfed
in flames.
Lowers your inhibitions, changes your intent,
Makes you do things that are too far gone to
mend.
Though it leads to remorse, though it leads to
regret,
As long as it teaches a lesson, the things you did
you won't forget.

Finally, there's that little butterfly,
Perched on your heart in shades of white.
She's so little but clutches on with feet of steel,
Her grasp unbreakable, the deepest wounds she
can heal.
In your worst, through the dark times, she keeps
you afloat,
Who is this little butterfly? – Her name is Hope.

A Heart's Change Of Mind

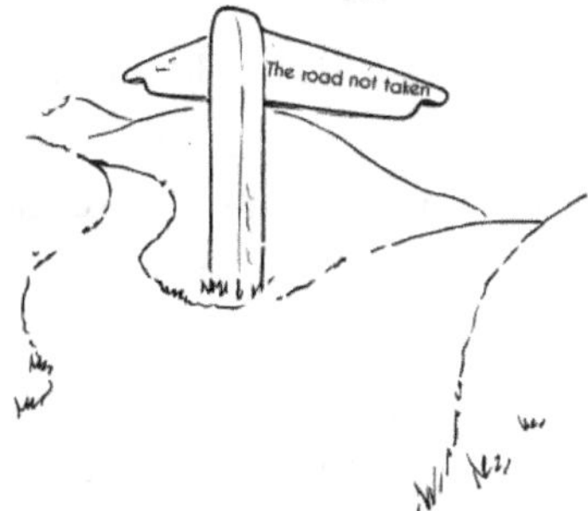

You used to know me so well,
Something changed inside me, was it after we
fell?
I remember you holding my heart in your arms,
Now it's gone, your arms encircling nothing to
protect from harm.

The moments that sent shivers up my spine,
Are now awkward instances that aren't anymore
mine.
Unsure of what turned that into this,
I sit here, pensive, as bright blue skies are
covered by a lasting eclipse.

Trying to make myself feel what I once did,
But those butterflies are long gone, and I was
just a kid.
And so these inky words bleed out of me,
Were we ever meant to last on empty promises
and guarantees?

A tear slides down my cheek; I know what I
must do,
But you were my whole world once, so how can
I do this to you?
You stayed by me when times were rough,
Showed me there's another path besides giving
up.

Your love healed those broken cracks in my
heart,
But now all that resides in me is a broken us, a
ripped-up piece of art.
You were my first love, but now I see you can't
be my last,
You still care so much, so how can I possibly
leave us in the past?

Someday, I will figure all of this out,
I just hope that I won't mutilate both our hearts
on the long fall down.

A Queen's Fist

I open my eyes, dark green flecked with gold,
My body taut with control as I sit upon my
throne,
My subjects bow before me, the room silent with
implications,
They don't dare meet my eyes, their faces tight
with anticipation.

I regally rise and pass them slowly, stride by
stride,
My calm movement and face a mask hiding the
turmoil raging inside.
As I move, a dagger slides into my hand,
I grip it firmly as I stand.

Quick as a panther, it flies from my palm into
the man next to me,
I don't spare him a glance; nothing competes
with my accuracy.
I stride forward, my face a porcelain mask,
This is me avenging the betrayal, not quite yet in
the past.
My gaze sweeps over their terrified faces,
I don't speak a word as the fire inside me blazes.

Another man falls down, lifeless and cold,
My brutal spirit so humiliated, my unassuming
wrist covered with gold
As I enact justice on the traitorous souls,
All for those who bled without reason, this grief
on me has an iron hold.

One body, then another, as the pile builds up,
All because they betrayed me, killing thousands
of those I loved.
Finally, I dismiss the remaining survivors,
My head steady, the flame inside me reduced to
embers.

Only when they leave does my mask break
apart,
My body convulses, my heart filling with
something so dark,

As I grieve the losses of my men and women,
My skin feels permanently stained with invisible
crimson.
I know what I did was needed to set an example,
If they ever again betrayed my kingdom, this
outcome was a sample.

But I never had dreamt of having to kill so
many,
Never thought that because of me, so many had
to be buried.
Yet I see that I couldn't have escaped it,
For a queen's role is to rule with compassion and
justice.

A Promise

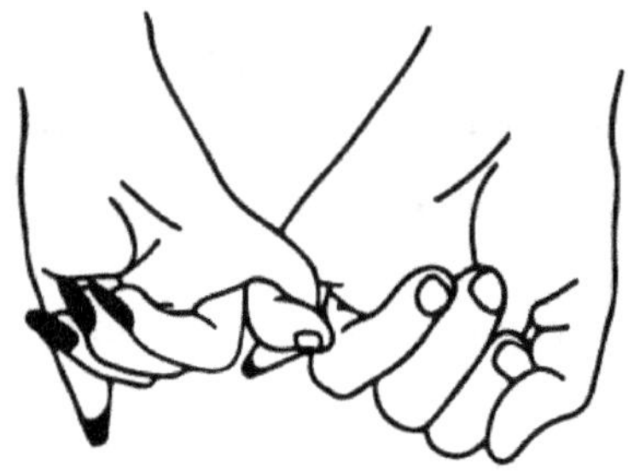

Such a small word, yet so strong,
With a promise, so many things can go wrong.
You make one in the spur of the moment,
Never realising that you get lifelong bound by it.
And then you forget, and break it so easily,
Later you feel regret, and you want to undo it
immediately.
Yet some things are impossible to reverse,
Even though you keep trying for months and
years.

So many types of promises are made,
One to stay by your friends each and every day.
To trust, care, and never give them up,
To always be there, even when the waters are
rough.

Another oath binding yourself to your lover,
To love them for who they are, and cherish each
moment together,
To keep them foremost in your heart and never
think selfishly,
Yet so many are broken by infidelity.

Then a vow to love your family,
The ones who gave you life, a solemn guarantee,
To never walk away, never forget the fact,
That every problem you got through in life,
without them you would've cracked.

And the most important promise of all,
The one you must keep, no matter in life how
hard the brawl,
Is the promise you make to your soul,
To be honest, good, and to love it so.

No matter the pain, no matter the strife,
You need to be kind to yourself, because in the
end, it's your life.

Broken Till She Isn't

I thought I knew the world,
One peek into its true nature and I hurled,
Never dreamt of its cold irony,
Never expected to be on my knees before it,
Nothing leaving my mouth but a desperate plea,
To get back the life I had lost,
To regain my mind from the day it had gone.
Never imagined the lengths people could go to,
Hardly thought they could make my vibrant
petals droop,
Didn't expect the betrayal and the hurt,
Never anticipated the knife in my back as soon
as I turned.

But still, my broken body stands straight,
Pain gripping me as my expressionless eyes
meet those glares of hate;
I hold my weary head up high,
Bracing myself for the inevitable fight;
Step by step my bruised feet force me to walk,
The world on the sidelines trying to crush me as
I hear its sarcastic applause;
The old me is gone, replaced with someone new,
An emotionless face indifferent to the body
attached to it, beaten black and blue;
I will not succumb to the agony I face,
After all, everybody knows that the world is not
a pretty place.

Blessed For The Lost

I lived my life knowing you would come,
You would come, take me to where everything
was numb,
I knew you, but never in person,
I heard of your soulless love, a black-and-white
version.
Your name, long whispered in factual myths,
They say you ruled with a caring heart and iron
fists.
They sing of your kingdom, blessed for the lost,
Your gentle darkness a cloak for all who had
crossed.

But now you have come to lead me away,
Lead me away to your land, where I will never
go astray.
You look me in the eyes, those bottomless pits of
black,

Filled with sympathy, it hardly seems like an
attack.
Your cold embrace envelops my body, so tired,
Your chill warming me, promising everything I
ever desired.
I let go of the days and hold your hand,
You were forever meant for me, always so stable
when nobody else can.

Oh Death, you have shattered me so,
Stealing my life but protecting my no longer
bruised soul,
Now your bloodless arms are all that I seek,
Your blindfolded company is all that I need.
I live without life, without a single breath,
Taken from the cruel world, you saved me, O
my saviour, O my Death.

ACKNOWLEDGEMENT

As this is my first time writing a book, and that too one being of poetry, acknowledgements are difficult to write. However, I do intend to show my gratitude to a number of people who have motivated me to reach the end, and those who believed in me when I didn't believe in myself.

To my mother, thank you for all your support and constant encouragement when I thought I couldn't do it. I could always talk to you when I needed help with anything, no matter what it was. All your advice and inspiration pushed me towards actually finishing my poetry.

To my father, you've always heard my ideas no matter what you were doing or what time it was. Thank you for the jokes and the attention.

To my teachers, who always pushed me into something I knew I would be happy doing, even when I was afraid. Your presence helped me write this.

And to all my friends, the closest ones as well as the acquaintances, you probably don't know it, but your lives, added to mine, gave me all the ideas I needed for various aspects of the world, and on living. An essential factor in writing this book was your presence in my life, the memories (both the good ones along with the ones that hurt), even those who were simply around me.

Thank you, all of you, for being there for me.